CIA
AGENTS

BY ABBY COLICH

CAPSTONE PRESS
a capstone imprint

Blazers Books are published by Capstone Press,
1710 Roe Crest Drive, North Mankato, Minnesota 56003
www.mycapstone.com

Library of Congress Cataloging-in-Publication Data
Names: Colich, Abby, author.
Title: CIA agents / by Abby Colich.
Description: North Mankato, Minnesota : Capstone Press, 2018. |
Series: Blazers. U.S. federal agents | Includes bibliographical references and index.
Identifiers: LCCN 2017039233 (print) | LCCN 2017044758 (ebook) |
    ISBN 9781543501469 (eBook PDF) | ISBN 9781543501421 (hardcover)
Subjects: LCSH: United States. Central Intelligence Agency—Juvenile literature. |
    Intelligence service—United States—Juvenile literature. | Espionage,
    American— Juvenile literature. | Spies—United States—Juvenile literature.
Classification: LCC JK468.I6 (ebook) | LCC JK468.I6 C616 2018 (print) |
    DDC 327.1273—dc23
LC record available at https://lccn.loc.gov/2017039233

Editorial Credits
Nikki Bruno Clapper, editor; Kyle Grenz, designer; Svetlana Zhurkin, media
researcher; Katy LaVigne, production specialist

Photo Credits
Getty Images: AFP/Mandel Ngan, 18–19, AFP/Tim Sloan, 21; Newscom: Danita
Delimont Photography/Dennis Brack, 16, KRT/Kansas City Star/Keith Myers, 26,
Zuma Press/Central Intelligence Agency, 6–7, Zuma Press/James Berglie, 28–29;
Shutterstock: Aleksandar Trifunovic, 14, Andrey Burmakin, 9, coka, 22, cunaplus,
23, Dusan Petkovic, 5, Gorodenkoff, 10, leungchopan, cover (front), Liderina, 25,
Panumas Yanuthai, 24, Rawpixel, 17, Sasa Kadrijevic, 13, sebra, 12

Design Elements by Shutterstock

Printed and bound in the USA.
042018   000436

Table of
Contents

The CIA

You live and work in another country. You use a fake name. You must get others to tell you secrets. You are a CIA officer. Your job is to get information for the **government**.

government—the group of people who make laws, rules, and decisions for a country or state

Just PART of the Job

Information the CIA gathers is called intelligence. It is often kept secret.

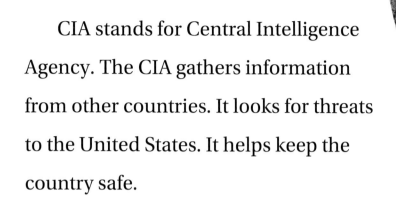

CIA stands for Central Intelligence Agency. The CIA gathers information from other countries. It looks for threats to the United States. It helps keep the country safe.

CIA building in Langley, Virginia

Working at the CIA

Getting a job at the CIA is not easy. Those who want a job wait up to a year to be hired. They must take a **polygraph**. They must pass a **background check**. These steps help show if someone can be trusted.

a man taking a polygraph

polygraph—a device used to detect if a person is lying by tracking changes in body functions

background check—the process of looking up and compiling information about a person

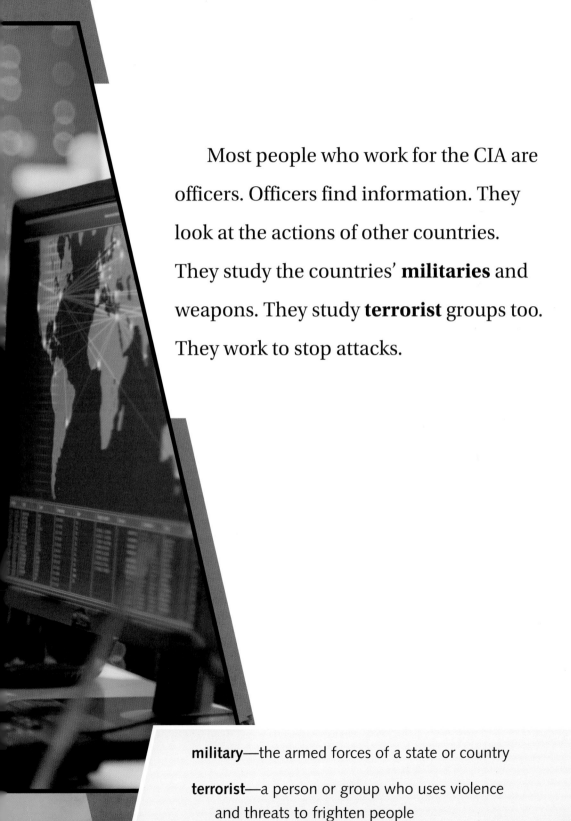

Most people who work for the CIA are officers. Officers find information. They look at the actions of other countries. They study the countries' **militaries** and weapons. They study **terrorist** groups too. They work to stop attacks.

military—the armed forces of a state or country

terrorist—a person or group who uses violence and threats to frighten people

Some CIA officers read and
watch news from other countries.
The news may have clues about
threats. Some officers are translators.
They translate the news into English.

Just PART of the Job

Satellites take pictures from space. The CIA looks for clues in the pictures.

satellite—a spacecraft used to send signals and information from one place to another

Just PART of the Job

Some people at the CIA make codes. The codes help keep information secret.

Some people at the CIA work with computers. They help stop **cyber** crimes. Others make tools that help the CIA spy. Some even work with **drones**.

cyber—having to do with computers and networks

drone—an unmanned, remote-controlled aircraft or missile

Just PART of the Job

Mapmakers work for the CIA. Their maps help **lawmakers** understand analysts' reports.

Analysts study information
gathered by officers. They
write reports. The reports go to
lawmakers. The lawmakers decide
how to keep the country safe.

Analysts must think and act fast. They decide if a threat is real. They choose what to tell lawmakers and when. Some analysts work with the president.

President Obama meets with the head of the CIA (far right) and other government leaders.

Going Undercover

Some officers work **undercover**.
The CIA gives them a new **identity**.
Few people can know the officers
work for the CIA. Often their friends
and family can't know about their job.

Just PART of the Job CIA officers learn
how to hide the truth
about their jobs. They
use cover stories.

Some CIA officers change their look
with fake body parts.

undercover—done in secret, especially in spying activities

identity—the things that make a person who he or she is,
such as a name, background, and job

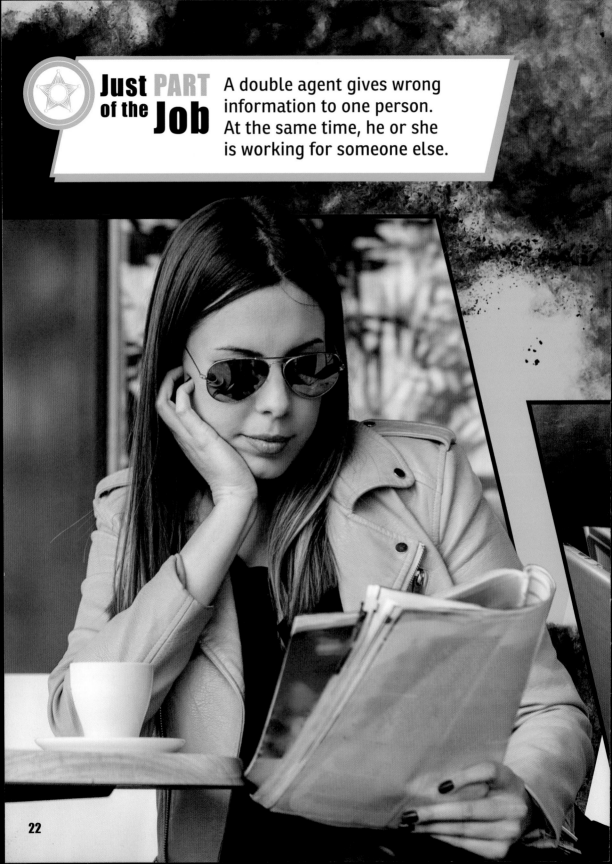

Just PART of the Job

A double agent gives wrong information to one person. At the same time, he or she is working for someone else.

Undercover officers spend years in another country. They often get a job there. The job may lead them to information they need. Officers also hire spies. These spies are called agents. They give information about their country to the officer.

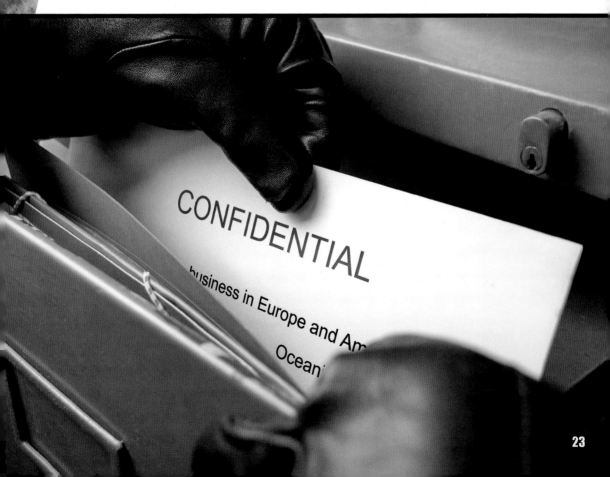

CONFIDENTIAL

business in Europe and Am

Ocean

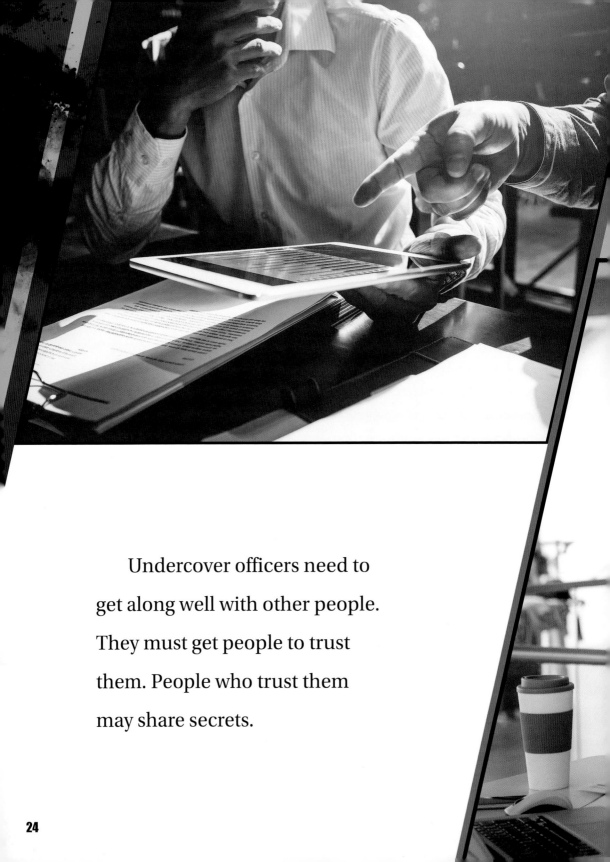

Undercover officers need to get along well with other people. They must get people to trust them. People who trust them may share secrets.

Just **PART** of the **Job**

Information that comes from people is called HUMINT. This is short for human intelligence.

This tiny camera is easy to hide.

Some officers plant hidden cameras. They hide listening tools. They may wear these tiny tools on their bodies too. No one can see them.

Just PART of the Job

The CIA made the "insectothopter" in the 1970s. This flying spy tool looked like a dragonfly.

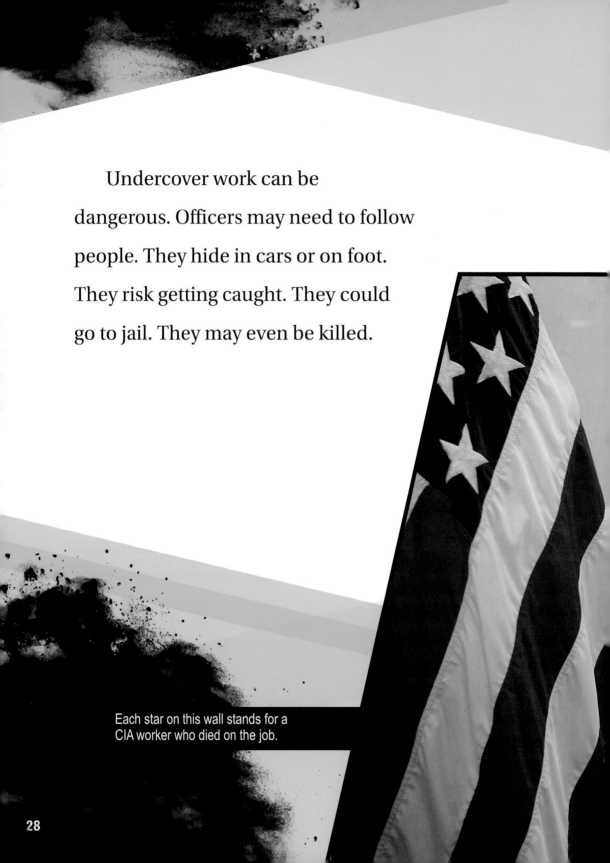

Undercover work can be dangerous. Officers may need to follow people. They hide in cars or on foot. They risk getting caught. They could go to jail. They may even be killed.

Each star on this wall stands for a CIA worker who died on the job.

Just PART of the Job

Most jobs at the CIA are very safe. Officers are rarely in danger.

IN HONOR OF THOSE MEMBERS
OF THE CENTRAL INTELLIGENCE AGENCY
WHO GAVE THEIR LIVES IN THE SERVICE OF THEIR COUNTRY

Glossary

background check (BAK-graund CHEK)—the process of looking up and compiling information about a person.

cyber (SY-buhr)—having to do with computers and networks

drone (DROHN)—an unmanned, remote-controlled aircraft or missile

government (GUH-vurn-muhnt)—the group of people who make laws, rules, and decisions for a country or state

identity (eye-DEN-ti-tee)—the things that make a person who he or she is, such as a name, background, and job

lawmaker (LAW-mayk-ur)—an elected official who makes laws

military (MIL-uh-ter-ee)—the armed forces of a state or country

polygraph (PAWL-ee-graf)—a device used to detect if a person is lying by tracking changes in body functions

satellite (SAT-uh-lite)—a spacecraft used to send signals and information from one place to another

terrorist (TER-ur-ist)—a person or group who uses violence and threats to frighten people

undercover (uhn-dur-KUHV-ur)—done in secret, especially in spying activities

Read More

Collard, Sneed B. *The CIA and FBI: Top Secret.* Freedom Forces. Vero Beach, Fla.: Rourke Educational Media, 2013.

Fraust, Daniel R. *A Career as a CIA Agent.* Federal Forces: Careers as Federal Agents. New York: PowerKids, 2016.

Murray, Laura K. *Spies in the CIA.* I Spy. Mankato, Minn.: Creative Education, 2016.

Internet Sites

Use FactHound to find Internet sites related to this book.

Visit *www.facthound.com*

Just type in 9781543501421 and go.

Super-cool stuff! Check out projects, games and lots more at **www.capstonekids.com**

Index